Trump, the Constitution & Training Within Industry

The Principles that made America Great

Table of Contents

Forward

This book explains the principles of Training Within Industry (T.W.I.) and the principles of a Top down management style (T.D.M.) If we understand the principles of T.W.I. as opposed to top down management, we will understand why there is such violent opposition to President Trump.
President Trump's way of doing things is based on the simple manufacturing principles that boosted American production in the second world war, or Training within Industry (T.W.I.).

The Principles are strong leadership at the top, and strong teams of workers who have a high degree of autonomy and resources to get the job done. There is a loyalty to staff, and an empowerment for leaders and workers to complete the details. The underlying belief is that the best leaders and workers are employed and they should be trusted to do the job. Interfering in the day to day running of an operation is counter productive. Leaders succeed when there workers succeed. This principle has worked in every industry to which it has been applied.

Democrats want a Government that controls every detail through regulation. Details must be controlled because leaders believe only they know what is best. There is a basic distrust of anyone in a position lower than they are. The top down approach allows for corruption and privilege for those in power. Free speech is allowed but only when it supports the beliefs of those in charge. Violence against opposition is accepted and encouraged.

This book shows how Presidents trump's statements link to the principles of lean manufacturing where managers achieve success by listening to and empowering workers .
The top down management style of Democrats has direct links to a top down management style.

The Book is in the format of A3 thinking - Every chapter is reduced to one page

"We have endorsed him because he is the only candidate who came and asked us what the situation really was, and what we actually needed."

Border Patrol Agents

1/ WW2 & Training Within Industry

During WW2, USA production reached an all time high. Productivity regularly increased by 100% -200% in industries that lost resources and skilled workers who were lost to the war. At the centre of the increase in production was train people to do the job. At the centre of all training were two questions that were always asked at every training session

a) Can this be done safer ?

b) Can this be done better ?

Team Leaders were trained on how to lead. They were instructed on how to get workers involved on what they were doing, and to actively seek input into the process.

The results were staggering. In one plant a bomber was built every hour. In another a liberty ship was built every day.

The principle of having people actively involved in the process and being free to make changes to the process was a winner.

An alternative name for this system is the Chaos theory which states that providing we have good leadership structures in place, order will always arise out of seeming chaos. During the 2016 election all the commentators were say "Trump cannot win because he does not have a ground game." What was really happening was Mr Trump held a rally, and people went out and did the work. There was no detailed organisation but people created their own organisation. This turned out to be more efficient and cheaper than the organisation of the Democrats which was a top down model.

The concept that having no organisation of details is often more organised and structured than having a highly organised system.

"When we work together as a team, there is nothing that we cannot achieve"

D.J.T.

2/ Then the Boys came home

When WW2 ended then men of the Armed Services returned. The concepts of Training within industry (T.W.I.) were replaced by the top down organisation of the Military. T.W.I. concepts were transferred to Japan which began to dominate the Auto and other industries. The Toyota way became the standard for effective management principles. When Executives of Toyota were asked where the principles came from they found an old dog eared book with notes all over it. It was the T.W.I. manual.

The principles of T.W.I. and top down management entered the political arena. The Democrats naturally favoured a top down management approach and regulations because they were the party founded by slave owners. The Republicans naturally favoured the T.W.I. approach of self reliance because they were the party who fought a war to abolish slavery.

In the 60's Democrats successfully re branded themselves and took credit for the advances in Civil Rights even though they voted against Civil Rights and 80% of Republicans voted for it. The Johnson amendment is an example of how Religious freedoms were under attack by the Democrats at the time of the Civil Rights movement.

The introduction of the Top Down management style into Government allowed systemic corruption. The media became part of the corrupt system and successfully lead a campaign to re-brand Republicans as racists, even though Republicans fought to abolish slavery and voted for Civil rights.
The media became part of the political system .

"You mean to tell me that those people walking down the street have more freedom than you to express themselves. If people like you cannot say what they think we need to get rid of the Johnson Amendment"
D.J.T. Speaking to Religious leaders at Trump Towers

3/ Employee Relations -The dog didn't bark Watson

With all the investigations into Candidate Trump, nothing significant in how employees of the Trump Organisation were treated was found. Candidate Trump reported that his employees had good healthcare and Education " Very Important" The Trump organisation has more women in Executive positions than men and they are paid more.

The T.W.I. model supports and values staff. It is a high wage model. During the war a large number of women and minorities were employed in industry. This changed after the boys came home.

Economically it makes sense to have a stable staff because costs of rehiring and training are avoided. Having a happy staff that come to work each day to improve the business has a huge economical benefit. Employing female executives also has a benefit because they are typically under employed and underpaid in other industries. Hiring women provides a better quality of employee that works harder. Equal opportunity is also a sound business practice because the best people are chosen for the job.

Question to Pastor Darrell Scott

"How can you support Donald Trump when he is a racist ?"

Answer

" When I walked into Trump Tower I saw Diversity. There were people from all races and religions. As I was walking with Mr Trump it was obvious that his people liked him and he knew all their names and talked to them directly. You cannot be a racist when you employ all these different people, they like you, and he know their names?

4/ Be loyal to your staff.

During the 2016 presidential campaign allegations were made against Corey Lewandowski Mr Trump was called upon by all sides to fire him. Corey was seen as a political liability.

The important aspect is that they were allegations. The concept of innocent until proven guilty did not apply. A characteristic of a top down management style is that principles only apply when they support management view. In political terms the constitution is quoted only when it supports the liberal view.

Mr Trump totally supported his manager. The underlying principle is clear. Managers and workers can only perform well when they a free to make mistakes. If they are worried about security of employment they will focus on not making mistakes. This will dramatically affect their performance, because they will do far less to avoid making mistakes. When Milania's speech writer made a mistake she was not fired.

A central theme in T.W.I. is " It the learner does not learn the instructor has not taught correctly." Good systems have safeguards built into them that minimise the effect of mistakes. The Japanese adopted the system as *Poke Yoke*. This involved changing the system so it is impossible to make a mistake. Staff are encourage to continually come up with improvements which are then fed back into the process. "Can this be done better? Can this be done safer."

"These are just allegations. I am not going to destroy a man's career because of unproven allegations. He has a wife and children"

DJT

5/ Work from First Principles – The Ice Skating rink

In the 1980 new York had spent 6 years and $13 million trying to renovate an old ice skating ring. The original quote was $4.7m and to be completed in two years They failed. Mr Trump offered to do the job for $3million dollars and in under six months. The actual cost was 25% under budget and 2 months ahead of schedule.

The secret was a simple question "Who builds the best ice skating rinks ?" He found the best people for the job and got them to do it. This is a basic T.W.I. principle. Provided we have the right people and structure in place we do not need to concern ourselves with every detail. The top down management approach is to have highly detailed planning with management acting as enforcement agents to ensure the work is done according to plan. If the plan is wrong all will fail.

The T.W.I. model would be to appoint someone who has successfully built an ice skating rink before. If they have successfully built 20 on time and budget then number 21 will also be on time and on budget. It is widely reported that Mr Trump talks to electricians and metal workers when he visits a site asking "What do you need to make the job better? What do you need to make the job safer ? "

" I could spend a million dollars on a report on how manufacturing is doing. It would take 9 months be 500 pages long and may not be accurate. Or I could ask a friend of mine who builds factories how things are going He told me that he is putting up large factories in Mexico the likes of which you have never seen. In USA not so good."

DJT Campaign Rally

6/ Focus on Safety Focus on Quality.

If we focus on Safety

- Safety goes Up
- Quality goes up
- Production Goes Up

If we Focus on Quality

- Safety goes up
- Quality goes up
- Production goes up

If we focus on Production

- Safety goes down
- Quality goes down
- Production goes down

If we use "the dog didn't bark Watson" theory, there are remarkably few claims of safety violations, or environmental breaches. The media has armies of reporters investigating every aspect of the Trump Organisation but have unearthed nothing statistically significant.

The effectiveness of regulations decrease as more are introduced. There is an optimum point between no regulations and over regulation. Moving away from the optimum point in either direction is detrimental. Top down management will always favour regulation because regulations control detail. T.W.I. companies will always seek the optimum point because they know that the most efficient companies are always the safest.

" We have to have regulations for Safety and the environment. It just that we have too many regulations that do not achieve what they are planed to do"

DJT on Regulations

7/ The Characteristics of Top Down management

- A small number of people make all the decisions
- Details of plans are controlled from the top
- Opinions of employees are neither sought or listened to.
- The structure is rigid and not open to change
- Organisations become unionised
- High staff turn over
- High sickness and absenteeism
- Departments become unionised
- Very low safety and efficiency records

When a Top Down Management style is applied to Government inefficiencies are inevitable. Programmes that are intended to help lose their effectiveness. Here are some figures

Under President Obama debt increased by $1,000,000,000,000 per year. Where are the benefits of debt? The debt is the result a top down management style. More Journalist have been prosecuted under President Obama than all of the previous Presidents combined. Top down managers always prosecute those who question their authority.

Top Down Education also fails. The programmes look good on paper but do not work. The reason is that each child has different experience, background and ability. Top Down education programmes fail because they assume that all children are the same. Unionisation of teachers is a symptom of a top down system. Giving parents a choice in the school their child attends works because parents know what school will best serve their child.

" We are going to send Education back to the States because parents know what is best for their children. I want every disadvantaged child to have a choice in the school they attend

DJT

8/ Why Obama Care was structurally unsound

Obama care was a top down management project. There were two inherent flaws.

The first was administrative costs. The first was that every one and every area was different. Obama care sought to introduce a fixed product into a market that was highly variable. This created the second structural fault. The cost of administrating a fixed program into a variable market meant that complex regulations were needed to adapt the program a a micro level. This in turn increased administrative costs till the program became unsustainable.

If each individual is given a choice in what type of insurance they buy the faults of Obama care are avoided. People buy what they need and there is no need to administer the program. Dabbawala is a person in India who collects food from a home in India and places it on a train. Another Dabbawala meets the train and transports the food to where the person works. The efficiency is that one mistake in 7,000,000 is made. The efficiency is because each transaction is between only 4 people, The cooker of meal,the first person to pick it up,the person to meet the train,and the person to receive the meal. Even though millions of meals are exchanged each transaction is between only 4 people. Negotiations are only between these 4 people.There may be variation in quality and costs within the system but these get resolved at the individual level.

When individuals are involved in their healthcare. The entire program is reduced to negotions between provider and patient which reduces costs, because people are only buying what they want. There will be variations but these variation will suit both patient and provider.

Car insurance is compulsory but not what type of car insurance or who it is bought from or what it covers.
" We want to be able to buy health care like I buy car Insurance. Across State Lines "

DJT

9/ Alcoholics Anonymous a comparison

In the 1920's Bill W. the founders of AA toured the US and talked to staff that worked in Factories. He sent reports on how the factories were performing to wall street and people bought stocks based on his reports. The principles of successful companies were later to appear in T.W.I.

As AA grew an organisational structure grew with in and a point was reached where no one would be able to become a member if the rules from every group were generally applied. AA was then organised along the lines of T.W.I. and the principles he observed in successful companies. A two paragraph statement read at every meeting. Each meeting had twelve steps on how thins were done – one page. Twelve traditions on how it was organised - one page. Each group was completely autonomous unless their actions affected AA as a whole.

The net result was that there are over 100,000 groups world wide. Each of these groups are almost identical in the way they operate, and AA has been running for over 80 years. Each groups runs on voluntary contributions which come to around $1.00 per member.

What confounds T.D.M. Is how such a large group arrive a a standard product with no linear organisation and control from the top. If the various AA offices in each count

ry disappeared each AA groups would continue and be unaffected.

The answer is that like T.W.I. and the US constitution provided a good vision and organisation is in place, people will always come up with a standard way of doing things if permitted to do so. There may be variation that is not meaningful in groups, some groups will fail, but overall AA continues to be successful.

"A.A., as such, ought never be organized; but we may create service boards or committees directly responsible to those they serve."

Tradition 9

10/ "The first casualty in war is the Truth"

"Its personal- They hate him They really hate him and its not going to change." Bill O'Reilly on Trump and the Media.

The resistance to President Trump is predictable and perfectly aligns with a Top Down management model. In general the media itself is a top down management structure. Many media icons consider themselves to be leaders. Any challenge to their authority must be crushed. If resistance increases, any means are justified.

Hard news has now become an opinion column. The heads of the organisations are the ones who decide what is important and slant reporting to fit their narrative. Reporters have become rabid dogs looking for anything to slay Dragon Trump. It matters not if the story is true or not, they will publish if anti Trump.

A T.W.I. style news organisation reports the truth and lets the audience make their own decisions.

The outcome of the war is easily predicted. All Top down organisations go through phases. They initially succeed and expand. To support their structures requires more administration. The organisation becomes inflexible as conditions change. The organisation then fails. As the media strives to enforce its position its customers will no longer trust the media. Customers will change channel or media types.

President Trump has more followers on Social media than any news organisation. The process of collapse has begun. Its like the boy who cried wolf. There have been so many lies the media is no longer believed. It is no coincidence that Bill O'Reilly and Tucker Carlson. They are reporting the news not making it, and viewers trust them.

> *"There is only one boss. The customer. And he can fire everybody in the company from the chairman on down, simply by spending his money somewhere else."*
>
> *Sam Walton*

11/ If you come up with an idea you must implement it

Often people come up with an idea or want something changed. A feature of T.D.M. it is other people who are expected to actually do the work. The T.W.I. approach is that we need have people doing the work not talking about doing it.

When T.W.I. was transferred to Japan a feature was planners and managers were required to work in the factories next to other workers. T.D.M. managers were horrified and considered it a waste of time to be away from their desks. The savings were that when managers were on the shop floor they could experience what the real problems were and address them.

In Chicago 4,000 mainly African Americans were shot in one year. The killing of African Americans did by other African Americans did not attract media attention. When an African American was shot by a policeman the media Falsely reported that he had been shot when he had his hands up. A group on a TV show were filmed with their hands up talking of an execution.

A lot of energy was spent on how bad the police were, but no actions by the protest to improve the situation were taken. Instead a charade of "Virtue Imaging" was staged. People protested to make themselves seem virtuous. In the mean time church leaders, athletes and others were working to improve life in the inner cities. One group wanted to look good, the other was actually doing things to improve the situation.

The concept of Virtue Imaging is a characteristic of T.D.M.. People say things to make themselves look smart or compassionate. The real compassionate people work unnoticed. One of the first meetings President Elect Trump had was with the Jim Brown who started the Ames-I-Can program.

"Its like a War Zone,Chicago is more dangerous than the wars we are fighting overseas. I will work with anyone who wants to improve the situation in the inner cities"

DJT

12/ Gemba Walks – What is real

T.D.M. managers sit in their offices and make plans. The education system itself is a T.D.M. structure. Education is America has become standardised so it produces students who are standardised. The critical issue is that the workplace is not standard.

As an example I was employed as a consultant to improve production in a bottling plant. Standard work had been introduced in an effort to introduced in an effort to get everyone to operate machines in the same way. Staff would not follow standard work plans and there were constant firings. The root cause of the problem was that the bottles and cartons that were being used in the plant were not in specification. The machine could not run correctly regardless of how they were set up. When the packaging quality improved all staff started to operate the machines the same way and production improved.

Unless we visit the workplace, we will be unable to find out what the real problems are. People will tell you what the issues are within the first two minutes of talking to them. Candidate Trump spent time talking to the people and they told him what the problems were. The political commentators talked to each other. Many still do not understand why he won. T.W.I. encourages talking to the workers. T.D.M. managers talk to each other and we have the Washington Bubble. For Trump opponents to accept that he won means that they have to accept their thought processes have been wrong. The typical T.D.M. response is to become more strident in opposition. Principles do not matter because we must *"Resist by any means"*

"My father would go to the work site and talk to the metal workers,the plumbers,the electricians. They are the ones that tell him what's really going and and what they need to get the job done. That's what he is doing now -Listening to the people
Eric Trump

13/ The Fascist left and Right -Two sides of a coin.

In the 1930's the brown shirts were beating their political opposition in Nazi Germany. Businesses that supported the Opposition were boycotted or attacked. Political meetings of the opposition were disrupted .The news actively worked with the press, and news was filled with propaganda much of which was "Fake News"

In the 2016 election liberal demonstrators were beating Trump supporters. Businesses that supported Trump were boycotted. Trump Rallies were disrupted. The news was filled with anti Trump propaganda. The media or "4th Estate" as reported by Wiki Leaks was working directly with the Clinton Campaign. Some protester were paid to disrupt Trump Rallies.

These two groups both hold the same public belief that a strong central Government that controls the activities of its people is needed for the good of all. Only the laws that supported their causes were followed. This is a T.D.M. approach. The methods of both groups are identical because they use the same approach. Though on the surface their ideals may seem different in reality they are very similar. Hillary's America by Dinesh D'Souza outlines the history of the Democratic party. He was prosecuted for making two illegal political donations by an Obama appointed prosecutor. This is the only example of such a prosecution in USA history.

The USA constitution is hold the same principles as T.W.I.. It allows for individual freedoms and limits the powers of Government. The fundamental principle is one of a decentralised Govt. That was why the war of independence was fought

We are going to Washington and we are going to Drain The Swamp.

DJT

14 A3 thinking – Effective meetings

A3 thinking originated in T.W.I., which used job cards to break each task into simple steps. These cards were independent and easily changed so improvements could be easily made.

If we take the example of building an Aircraft, the basic steps were outlined in a plan. The basic order was controlled and relatively inflexible. The details of how the work was done was controlled by job cards. The work was highly standardised, but very easily changed or improved. Workers had a direct means of controlling how the job was done.

Meetings were used to assign people to actions. They were not used to solve problems. They were used to assign people to solve problems. Before a meeting is held the principals will hold one on one meetings with those who will be attending the meeting to gain agreement on a topic. When the meeting is held agreement has already been agreed upon before hand.

On the surface this may seem inefficient but if we look at the numbers this is a very efficient system. If there are 10 people at the meeting the pre meeting would take 10 Min or 100 Min total. The main meeting would take 15 Min or 150 Min total. The sum of the time to reach agreement is 250 min. The traditional meeting may take 60 Min or 600 Min total and agreement may not be reached.

This is why Congressional hearings are so inefficient. They have hearings but few decisions. Open meetings encourage divide and hardening of positions. Private meetings allow for an exchange of views and compromise because there is no audience.

" This has been a great day. This is the first time I can remember Union leaders being invited into the Oval Office to hear what we had to say. I am very encouraged.

Union Leader

15/ Rewards and recognition

T.D.M. will formalise rewards. There will be incentive bonuses, employee of the month, holidays and all manner of goodies. These generally are individual rewards designed to improve performance by rewards. These schemes have two flaws. They assume that employees will only perform if they are given incentive and individuals are rewarded. The net result is that team members are in completion with each other and team work is not promoted..

The T.W.I. model assumes that the work itself will be rewarded and the pay packet is the reward The T.W.I. model recognises individual efforts. Teams are rewarded if an individual comes up with and idea or special performance. The net result is that team members want each other to succeed because they all benefit.

Typical recognitions are thank you, and verbally recognising performance. If a manager visits the work place and talks to the workers and shows interest this will improve production. This relates to the Gemba walk.

T.D.M. sees workers are part of the process and the process is improved when workers do their jobs better Safety is achieved by better awareness and care by the workers.. T.W.I. sees workers as individuals and the process is improved when workers devise ways to improve the process. Safety is improved by making the process safer.

One noticeable feature of President Trump is the number of times he thanks people and verbally acknowledges someone doing a good job. There is a constant stream of people visiting the white house with regular meetings to assign actions

" I would like to thank ------ " " Its not me its all of us I cannot do this without the help of all of you "

DJT

16/ T.D.M. v the USA Constitution

At the time of the American War of Independence, the King of England and his officers controlled the Colonies of America. The king used his powers to to maintain rule. This was a top down management style. Corruption and abuse of power became entrenched, and a war was fought so the citizens could choose for themselves what the laws should be. " Government for the people by the people."

The basic principle of the Constitution was there were things that could only be done by the United States such as defence,building roads bridges etc. There were other things that should be left to individuals to decide. The constitution limited the powers of Govt. and what it could do. A balance was set between Govt. powers and the rights of individuals.

T.W.I. says that the broad direction is set by management and the details are left to individuals. In many organisation management creep starts and the organisation becomes over organised. Gradually more managers are appointed that belief that they know what is best because they are educated in a T.D.M. system. The system works well for a while then the organisation starts to fail.

The same thing happens in Govt. Power is transferred to Washington and the bureaucrats assume power and trade favours. What is happening is 2017 is the second War of Independence, this time it is a rebellion against the bubble in Washington. The media is part of the bubble. Resistance to change is essential for the bubble for their position is under attack, even though they have no right to the position

" There are over 300,000 laws and regulation, the breaking of which result in imprisonment. W are unable to count them We are always trying to strike a balance between too many laws and not enough Laws. We always try to find the Golden Mean"

Neil Gorsuch

17/ Govt. Bureaucracy T.D.M. v T.W.I.

One regulation leads to another. Top down managers need administrators to enforce rules. As the number of administrators grow so does the need for more regulations to control the administrators and so it grows. A point is then reached when the administrators start to create their own regulations, which create more administrators. The point is reached where over 300,000 laws and regulations are created which result in imprisonment.

Obama care requires an army of administrators. However if each transaction is between the patient and Doctor, there is no need for regulation. A situation arises like the Dabbawala in India where with no regulations the most efficient distribution system in the world is in place.

Beauracrates and Top down managers find this concept intolerable. It challenges everything they have been taught and practiced. They the product of a T.D.M. education, reinforced by a T.D.M. media, working in a T.D.M. structure.

President Trump challanges the very existence of the bureaucrats . Their livelyhood, privilege, and power are under threat so they must fight "By any Means"

Many Trump supporters witnessed the transfer of resources to the bureaucrats. They saw their taxes and freedom, to Washington. They staged a rebellion. They ignored the media and political class and adopted the Sam Walton mantra. The voter is King they can change the Govt. by taking their vote somewhere else.

The established order including Hollywood repeated the mantra of "He is a Racist, woman hater, a Nazi " and ignored any evidence to the contary.

"There is a principle which is a bar against all information, which is proof against all argument, and which cannot fail to keep a man in everlasting ignorance. This principle is, contempt prior to examination. "

William Paley

18/ T.D.M. Hypocrisy alive and well with rebranding

Followers of T.D.M. Have one characteristic.Laws and principles are only applied when they suit their cause. They make extensive use of rebranding. They present one idea then act the opposite

- ***"Build Bridges not walls"***- The hollywood elite live in gated compounds. They want refugees and immigrants but not to live in their neighborhood.
- They protest against fossil fuels yet drive fossil fuel powered cars and boats to protests.
- They protest about the environmental impact of pipe lines and leave their protest camps with tons of garbage for others to clean up.
- Beat up political opponents but claim to be for justice
- Decry President Trump for criticizing the media as an attack on free speech when it his right to free speech that he is exercising.
- Want open borders and immigration but do not want any immigrants living in their neighborhood.
- Are against the police until they themselves are a victim of crime.
- Are against school choice while their own children can go to the school of choice.
- The media host who said she would not host Melania Trump " Why would I host her, she doesn't even speak English " At the same time she was berating President Trump as being anti Immigrant

The above are examples, are how T.D.M. thinkers manipulate the truth to appear to be virtuous - Virtue Imaging

"The true hypocrite is the one who ceases to perceive his deception, the one who lies with sincerity."

Andre Gide

19/ Jim Brown The true Activist

Jim Brown is doing it. His activism is of a practical kind. He has used is position to improve the lives of his fellow Amer-I-Cans by starting a foundation to practically improve lives of people in inner cities. This requires effort by himself and others. Activism is not talking about things but actually doing them.

A feature of Top Down thinking is that the elite make statements and expect others to do the work. The underlying thought pattern is a belief in their intellectual elitism. They consider what they think and do to be superior to those around themselves. This translates into Virtue imaging where they take popular stands to show everyone what a virtuous person they are. An example is someone turning up at a soup kitchen and having photos taken of them "helping" The effort is brief and the real work is left to the real activists who were doing the work before and after the Celebrity leaves.

When Jim Brown met with President Elect Trump he faced sever criticism by others. The Gist of the criticism was that the inner city problem could only be solved by Democrats. Jim Brown said " I will meet with and work with anyone who wants to help." This is true activism, wanting to bring about change. The measure of success is improving the situation

To the Democrats who would not attend the inauguration,the Black Caucus who would not met with the President, The Media who mount constant attacks. If you are successful in stopping President Trump you measure of success will be how badly you have damaged the country and those you proport to represent.

"Money has changed today's black athletes. Those who have the ability as African men to bring a change in a community that so desperately needs it are concentrating only on their own careers, some charities and how much money they can make."

Jim Brown

20/ How President Trump will succeed.

This is the accepted blueprint to effect change.

- – Create a Vision **Complete**
- – Communicate the vision **Complete**
- – Select the best leaders to complete the Plan **Complete**
- – Give the leaders complete autonomy to complete the task **Complete**
- – Form alliances with those who share a similar view **Complete**
- – Work in areas of agreement **Complete**
- – Include others in the vision **Complete**
- – Get early wins **Complete**
- – Win Over Sceptics **Work in Progress**

There is nothing magical in creating change. The above steps are those adapted in all successful change programmes.In the end success will come overnight after 2 years of hard work.

It is the system that needs to be changed. Changing the people in the system does not effect change. Barack Obama championed change and won elections on the need to change.

In the end people changed but the system did not. Hope and promise dissipated like smoke in the wind. "Change will not come if we wait for some other person or some other time. We are the ones we've been waiting for. We are the change that we seek" Barack Obama

USA is returning to the principles that worked well in the past The Constution and Training Within Industry

"At any stage in change, it's always worth reflecting on what has worked well in the past, in similar circumstances."
                                                                    Ian Saunders

Other Books by Author

" Standard Operating Procedures made easy-Write to Unit Standards"

"Eliminate Noise Hazards a Lean Six Sigma Approach"

"Environmental Noise Control"

" Make Great Inductions "

"Measure noise with Smart Phones "

"Fishermans Lies" CD and Book

"Tuapeka Ferry" CD and Book

www.ingramcontent.com/pod-product-compliance
Lightning Source LLC
Chambersburg PA
CBHW070838310526
45788CB00017B/2078

* 9 7 8 1 5 4 4 7 5 1 4 0 5 *